Couponing Basics

Pam Hill

CONTENTS

1

Benefits of Using Grocery Coupons - How Grocery Coupons Can Save You Money

The use of grocery coupons clearly divides the shopping public in two. There are those who think using grocery coupons are just too much work for very little savings while others simply cannot go to the store without them. There are even some who cannot live without grocery coupons due to the unemployment rate and the increasing cost of living! But the bottom line is if you want to stretch your budget, have more food on your table and items on your pantry, and save money each time you head at the checkout counter, then use grocery coupons.

Never mind what other shoppers say or think. If they want to waste their money buying at regular prices and do away with discounted rates and have stores and manufacturers vacuum their salary at the cashier is completely their choice. If they do not want to be wise with their money, so be it. As for you, realizing the value of grocery coupons will definitely take you a long way. Sure, it may take some amount of effort getting coupons and organizing your coupons and shopping trips, but it also takes effort to earn money. It is always better to spend it wisely than waste it all and worry later about needing to make some more.

This is the beauty of grocery coupons. What used to be a fixed expense becomes smaller and smaller each and every time as you get better with your use of the coupons. Some may say the amount that you save with each coupon is pennies or a dollar but even a tiny speck of sand can bury a house if it piles on up eventually. For example, for your grocery trip this weekend, you have collected two $1 coupons for cereal, four $0.50 ones for tooth paste, and another $1 off a bottle of peanut butter. This alone rakes you $5 in savings at the counter. Without the coupons, this is $5 more you are spending. Naturally, if you practice and work on your use of grocery coupons, you will have more coupons on hand and you will be able to increase your discounts and keep more money in your pocket.

Coupons are really money in your pocket. A good way to stay motivated in using them is thinking of them this way. If you have a $2 coupon, do not look at it as a piece of paper but as $2 cash on your hand because that is really what it is. It easily converts and it can truly do a lot of good for your finances. Over time, it takes a snowball effect. The more you save on your groceries, the more money you will have to spend on other utilities, bills, and responsibilities. You will have more money for the mortgage, more for the electricity bill, more for home improvements, even more for your kid's allowance. These big benefits all come from the simple change that you made on your grocery shopping by using coupons.

Clearly, there is no doubt how big grocery coupons are and how much they are worth. Considering the fact that you do get them for free is already a big plus and big value. By starting the coupon habit today you can start helping yourself buy your financial freedom. Money and shopping do not always have to cause you major stress and no matter how much you earn, savings in your pocket is always a great thing and it is very easy to do with grocery coupons so pick up the habit and reap the rewards.

And now print free grocery coupons, just click here... http://couponcoach.com/

It is simple to get free coupons and save at your local grocery store. Learn how to maximize your grocery savings and print free coupons, just click here... http://couponcoach.com/
By Tammie Johnson

2

WANT TO START COUPONING?

Here is a basic introduction to the world of couponing. Most of us have heard of or seen the show Extreme Couponing, and wonder if you can do the same thing; well, you can. The more time and effort you spend on couponing, the more money you can save. The purpose of this article is to get you familiar with the 3 Steps to Couponing and save you as much time and effort as possible when starting on your journey in the world of couponing. This article was written for Canadian couponers, but the steps are the same, regardless of country.

Every week there are items you can get for free (or extremely cheap) by combining a great sale with a good coupon.

1. COLLECT... There are many different ways to acquire coupons. Here are some of the various sources: call or e-mail companies to request them, from flyer inserts found in some newspapers, from tear pads found in stores, from "peelie" sticker coupons found on products. from cereal boxes or other products that have coupons inside their packaging, from your dentist (yes your dentist), from online sites that will mail them out, printable coupons, from magazines, etc.

2. ORGANIZE... and sort your coupons so that when you need to locate them, they are easily found. There are many ways to do this. The most common seems to be a binder

with baseball card sleeves in it. But you can also use envelopes, baggies or an accordion file.

3. WAIT... for a sale. Look out for your local flyers and compare sale prices with the coupons you have. You can usually get an item each week for free (provided you have "collected" the right coupons!). Typically an item will go on sale (a really good sale) about every 3 months... So the idea is to stock up on a 3 month supply.

It is a good idea to print off the Coupon Policies for the stores that you are planning to shop at (and keep these policies with your coupons, for your reference).

Please keep in mind some basic couponing etiquette to make your couponing experience a good one. 1) Only use coupons for the items and products specified. 2) When collecting coupons from tear pads, don't take the entire pad (save some for the next couponer) 3) When purchasing multiples of the same item, don't clear an entire shelf (if the person before you did this, there would be none for you).

For more information, check out www.ChallengerShop.com [http://www.ChallengerShop.com].

This article was written using information provided by ChallengerShop.com.

Article Source: http://EzineArticles.com/expert/Joel_A_Berstecki/1268204

3

Couponing: 10 Tips for Getting Started

Perhaps you've seen one of those television shows wherein a shopper uses an incredibly large amount of coupons to bring her grocery bill down to just a few dollars and cents at checkout. "If I can do it, anyone can do it!" this person exclaims, and we do want to believe her. Who wouldn't want to save money at the food store? However, the people who save the most money generally spend quite a bit of time gathering coupons, organizing them and strategizing their shopping trips. Getting the kind of savings by using coupons that you see on TV may not be possible right away (and you may not have quite as much time to invest in couponing), but using coupons will save you money. Start small and then build up as your schedule and desire permit. Use the following 10 tips as your guide to making coupons pay:

1. Pick a store. Choose the food store that you most often shop at to focus your couponing skills on first. It can be too overwhelming for a novice couponer to keep track of all the sales at all the stores in their area and coordinate trips to all of them. Usually, stores also have a minimum purchase amount to obtain sale items.

2. Familiarize yourself with your store's coupon policy. Every store has its own rules regarding coupons. Stay up-to-date on the store's rules and you avoid wasting your

time planning purchases around coupons that your store will not honor.

3. Sign up for coupon websites. Open a free email account just for this purpose. If you search "couponing," some of the top sites should come up. Join their mailing lists to receive free, printable coupons. Also join sites for products that you use regularly and know you'll be buying. These companies appreciate brand loyalty and regularly offer coupons for their products on these sites; diapers, cereal and laundry detergent are just a few that come to mind.

4. Have a simple system. Most serious couponers have large, impressive-looking binders jam-packed with coupons in clear plastic sleeves--leave these systems for the future couponing you. Just starting out, all you really need is a small accordion file or plain envelopes (whichever you already have on hand will do). Don't make the mistake of spending your future coupon savings on today's coupon organization system.

5. Link your system to your store. Use one file slot or one envelope for every aisle in your chosen store. File your coupons according to aisle and also write your shopping list by aisle. Keep one envelope or file slot open for the coupons you know ahead of time that you'll be using, but always bring all of your coupons with you every shopping trip.

6. Start clipping. If you're already receiving coupons with your newspaper, start with those. Perhaps a friend, relative or neighbor has coupon inserts that they don't

want or need. If you choose, you may want to start purchasing the Sunday paper for the coupon inserts. However, if you're just getting started, don't buy multiple copies of the paper for the inserts or coupons from a clipping service. If you do not make use of these extra coupons, then you've wasted money instead of saving it. The coupons you will have on hand just from the paper and from the web will be enough to get you started.

7. Stick to a schedule. Choose one day/evening a week to "work" on couponing, i.e., clipping coupons, printing coupons from websites, filing, checking your store's circular, etc. This ensures that you'll never miss a great deal.

8. Keep track of your time. Be sure to note exactly how much time you're spending on couponing and shopping and compare this time spent to the amount that you spent just on shopping alone. This gauge can help you decide if using a lot of coupons is worth your time and effort.

9. Keep track of your savings. This combined with tip no. 8 will help you to decide whether or not coupons pay for you. If you're really not saving that much money and spending more time than you'd like trying to, maybe couponing isn't for you.

10. Purge regularly. Nothing is more frustrating than having a great coupon (which will double!) matched to a great store sale item, only to find out at checkout that this great coupon has expired! Incorporate a check of expiration dates into

the schedule that you have established to be sure that this never happens. Keeping coupons in order of oldest to newest (within their respective file) can also help.

Article Source:

4

7 Of The Best Places To Find Coupons

If you're a bargain shopper, you probably love to use coupons too. Getting the best deal is important, especially these days with the ups and downs of grocery prices. You never know when the prices will change, and it's best to get the lowest price you can. On top of that, any coupon added is a bonus for you. Coupons are just like money, money that you don't have to work for that is. Less money paid at the grocery store is more money in your pocket. Here are a few places to get coupons:

Here are some of the best places to find coupons:

1. Sunday Newspaper- Having the Sunday newspaper delivered to your home is one of the best places to get coupons. If you look for the largest newspaper in your city or state, you can usually find a deal by calling the sales office to get a promotional rate for the best deal. If you have the newspaper delivered, you won't miss all the great coupon deals.

2. Multiple Newspapers- Newspapers are recyclable. And if you think of what you get out of purchasing more newspapers, you can really come out ahead. Depending on how many coupons you get from each paper, many could be doubled depending on the particular store you shop at, by the time you're done

clipping coupons, you're bound to come out ahead.

3. Manufacture's Websites- Most people have their favorite brands of grocery items. Sending an email or letter directly to the manufacturer letting them know how much you enjoy their products is another way to get more coupons. In return, most companies will send out coupons to customers. Even if you're not happy with a particular product, companies tend to send you coupons just as a gesture of goodwill and to further their customer service.

4. Product Packaging- Lots of products come with a coupon inside or outside the box, or even inside the label. I've missed them at times not realizing they were there.

5. Direct Mail- Retailers like to encourage shopping and will include coupons to encourage you to shop at their store. Watch for these in the mail and be careful when you're sorting your junk mail.

6. In-Store Displays- Many products have instant savings with coupons located on the shelf next to the item featured. If the item is on sale, you'll get an even bigger savings. And if not, you can save it for when it goes on sale. This way you'll save even more.

7. Printable Coupon Sites- Printable coupon sites are a great resource for extra savings. Make sure you check these out for your list of items. There are multiple sites, so give them a look.

These are just a handful of places to check when in search of coupons for a better deal. It really does make a difference in the bottom line of your grocery bill. I love to save money and I love to find bargains.
Happy Shopping!

Article
Source: http://EzineArticles.com/expert/Mandye_Mason/948538

5

Grocery Coupon Organization Basics

ORGANIZING YOUR COUPONS

Cutting coupons from a paper, mailer or magazine or printing them from a website is of little benefit to you if you don't organize your coupons so that you can find the coupon you need or if you don't even know you have that coupon. There are many ways to organize your coupons; you need to find the one that works well for you and one you will continue to use.

Several basics to get you started:

Develop a coupon filing system You can organize by category--dairy, frozen foods, cereal, canned foods etc. You can organize by aisle (this works best if you shop mainly at one store. This method is also the better option if you take your coupons with you to the store and discover unadvertised sales for which you might have a coupon). You can also sort your coupons by date. This method, however, requires you to sort through all your coupons each trip to the store. (More details on organizing your coupons are listed in the next section).

Determine what you will keep your coupons in You can use a shoe box or a coupon wallet to start out. However, if you get serious about couponing, you will soon find you need an accordion folder or a notebook (or several notebooks) with slotted sleeves to sort your coupons by whatever method you have settled on using. If you use the accordion folder (or a box), you will also need envelopes to sub divide you coupons by your chosen method.

Sort and file your coupons as soon as possible The more organized you are, the more money you will save. The more organized you are, the easier couponing is. Therefore, it is important that you file your coupons (either the ones you cut out or the ones that you print out) soon after you acquire them so that they don't get misplaced or thrown away. It is also much easier to sort and file as you go, rather than attack a huge pile of coupons all at once.

Remove expired coupons on a regular basis Expired coupons don't save you money and they make finding the coupons you need more difficult. Set a schedule for removing expired coupons and stick to it.

COUPON FILING SYSTEMS

One of the first things you need to do is decide what type of system you will use for sorting and organizing your coupons. You need to decide on which filing system best suits your personality and style. The purpose of coupon organization is so you will know where to find a particular coupon and to help you make use of that coupon before it expires. If you try one system and it doesn't work for you, try another. The key is to find one that works best for your personality and that you will consistently use. Bottom line: If you do not effectively organize your coupons, you will not save as much money and you will be less likely to continue couponing.

Alphabetically by product name (i.e. Kellogg's or Kraft). Simply put, you sort your coupons by name A-Z. The biggest problem with this method is remembering how you sorted them. For example, did you sort the Kellogg's Frosted Flakes coupon under K for Kellogg's or F for Frosted Flakes? Did you sort the Kraft Macaroni & Cheese by K for Kraft or M for Mac & Cheese? If you choose this method you must determine how you will classify your coupons (by manufacturer or actual product name) and consistently follow that decision. If you are brand or product loyal, this method works well.

Alphabetically by product type (i.e. Cereal or Laundry Detergent). Again, this is a simple method of sorting A-Z. If you are not brand or product loyal (and to take fullest advantage of coupons you shouldn't be), sorting your coupons by product type, rather than product name makes it easy to save money. For example, you need cereal. If you sort this way, you can search and see if any of your coupons match up with a product on sale. Our kids prefer Cocoa Krispies and Cap'n Crunch but if we have a coupon for Cheerios and it's on sale, we buy Cheerios that week. It is also easier to remember to put the Frosted Flakes coupon under C for Cereal than it is to remember if you put it under K for Kellogg's or F for Frosted Flakes.

Alphabetically by Product category (i.e. Health and Beauty or Dairy or Canned Goods). If you use this method, you will clearly have fewer categories to sort into and some people prefer that. The problem with this method is that, because you have fewer categories, you have many more coupons to sort thorough to look for a particular product or product type. For example, if you need soap and it's in your HEALTH & BEAUTY section, you will have to sort through coupons for make-up, shampoo, Q-tips etc. to find the soap coupons. You also have to remember how you categorized a product. For example, did you put the aluminum foil under BAKING (for example) or did you put it under PAPER PRODUCTS? Did you put the coupons for Ziploc bags under GENERAL GROCERY or SNACKS or PAPER PRODUCTS?

By Expiration date. When sorting coupons by expiration date, you file by the month the coupon expires. For example, you put all your coupons expiring in December together; all those in January together, etc. Using this method makes it much more difficult to find particular coupons as you have to sort through every coupons each shopping trip. However, using this method does make it easier to cull your expired coupons.

By Aisle. When using this method, you sort your coupons by the aisle the product is found on in the store. This method works best for those who shop mostly at one store although many stores have essentially the same layout. Sorting coupons by aisle works really well if you decide to take your coupons to the store with you. You may also find it helpful when sorting by aisle or by expiration date to set up subcategories of similar products to make finding the coupons easier.

By Insert. There are two major coupon inserts that come in the paper: RedPlum and SmartSource. A lot of couponers prefer not to cut their coupons until they are going to use them. When you get an insert, it will have a date on it. You put all the RedPlum inserts together, sorted by date, and each of the SmartSource inserts together, sorted by date. This method works especially well if you use an on-line website that matches up sales at particular stores with coupons that are available. For example, a site may tell you that Oscar Mayer hot dogs are on sale at your favorite store and that there is a 50 cents off coupon for Oscar May hotdogs in the RP (RedPlum) circular dated 11/12/11 (just a random date for example purposes). You just go to your Redplum inserts, find the one with the correct date and cut out the coupon at that time. In our opinion, if there is a website that provides this information for the store(s) you shop at, this is, by far, the easiest (and best) method to use.

If you choose to file by insert, you will also want to select one of the other methods for organizing your printable coupons. We know many people only print coupons when they are going to use them right away but we suggest you scan the printable sites weekly, print coupons that you feel you will use and file them away.

Regardless of the coupon organization system you choose, you must make sure to cull your expired coupons regularly. Removing the expired coupons will make finding the coupons you need much easier and reduce the frustration of missing a deal because you couldn't find a coupon you just knew you had.

Article Source: http://EzineArticles.com/expert/James_Dooley/1213860

6

How To Save Money By Checking Grocery Store Ads Each Week

Shopping for groceries can be expensive. It's even more expensive if you don't pay attention to the cost of what you are buying. There are ways to save money on the groceries you purchase. All it takes is a little time and some organization and you will be on your way to big savings.

Here is a list of ways you can save money at the grocery store by shopping the sale ads each week:

1. Start by getting the sale flyers from each of the grocery stores in your area. In most areas, these flyers come every week in the mail. You may have thrown this out in the past and thought it was junk mail. Be sure to start saving them because you will need to do some prep work before you get to the grocery store.

2. When you have gathered all the flyers, start going through them one at a time. Take a sheet of notebook paper and make a list of the items you see that are on sale that you need from the sale flyers. Include both the item name (including brand) in one column and the price in a second column. That way when you get to the store, you will know the specific brand to look for as well as what the price should be. If you find something

at the store that isn't marked with the sale price, be sure to have the cashier do a price check before you buy the item.

3. If you are out of something, but don't see it on sale, decide if you can wait another week to see if it goes on sale again or if you want to purchase it now. If it is not on sale but you need it, consider buying another cheaper brand or the generic version.

4. Once you have your list made for each store, add up the total for each store. Is the total of these numbers within your budget? If not, remove some items that you don't need this week until you are within your budget.

5. If you do not have time or don't want to shop at multiple stores, look for the store that has the best prices on the most items you know you will use and plan to shop at that store for the week.

6. Don't just buy something because it's on sale! If you don't like it, it will just end up going to waste and even though it was on sale, you didn't really save anything if it gets thrown out.

Remember that most sales rotate every 3 months or so, depending on the store. I find it helpful to keep a list of things I am out of as I use them up so I can use that list when I'm looking at the sales flyers. That way I don't forget things I'm out of and have to pay full price for it later.

If you want to take that savings one step

further, match the grocery sale ads each week to coupons. This is where you really will start to see big savings.

Jenny Kerr is an expert author, consultant, blogger and social media professional. She loves living a flexible lifestyle and spends most of her time reading, gardening and trying new recipes she has cooked from scratch. Jenny is passionate about helping people save money and blogs about it on her Jenny Pincher site. She has taught her self-developed "Basics of Budgeting" course throughout the St. Louis area. Visit her site http://thejennypincher.com/ to get her free eBook and Single Girl's 7 Day Budget program. You can also find more information on http://thejennypincher.com/debt/budget-help/coupon-resources/

Article Source: http://EzineArticles.com/expert/Jenny_Kerr/646436

7

Store Coupon Policies

Walmart Coupon Policy

General Coupons Policy

• Use of 40 or more coupons requires manager approval.

• There are no limits on multiples unless specified in the ad. One coupon per item allowed.

Double Coupons Policy

• Walmart does not double coupons.

Competitor Coupons Policy

• No competitor's coupons are accepted but Walmart does price match.

Internet Coupons Policy

• Walmart accepts Internet printable coupons as long as they scan.

Rainchecks Policy

• Rainchecks are issued at Walmart, per the statement on the back of the weekly ads. Some items are not eligible for rain checks including "while supplies last" and "bonus" items.

Target Coupon Policy

Double Coupons Policy

• Coupons are redeemed at face-value only (no doubling).

Stacking Coupons Policy

• Target accepts one (1) manufacturer coupon and one (1) Target store coupon for the same item (unless prohibited by either coupon).

• Coupon amount may be reduced if it exceeds the value of the item after other discounts or coupons are applied (no cash back).

Internet Coupons Policy

• Target accepts valid Internet coupons that have a scannable bar code.

• The store will not accept Internet coupons for free items with no purchase requirements.

Competitor Coupons Policy

• Target will not accept competitor coupons.

Buy One, Get One Free (BOGO) Coupons Policy

• BOGO coupons cannot be combined (i.e. you cannot use two BOGO coupons on two items and get both for free). Unless stated otherwise on the coupon, the use of one Buy One Get One Free coupon requires that two of the valid items are presented at checkout of which one item will be charged to the guest and the 2nd item will be discounted by its full retail price.

- If a Target BOGO coupon is used, one additional manufacturer coupon may be used on the first item.

- If a Manufacturer BOGO coupon is used, one additional Target coupon may be used on the first item.

Walgreens Coupon Policy

General Coupons Policy

• The number of manufacturer coupons, including Register Rewards manufacturer coupons, may not exceed the number of items in the transaction. The total value of the coupons may not exceed the value of the transaction.

Double Coupons Policy

• Walgreens does not double coupons.

Stacking Coupons Policy

• Walgreens accepts one (1) manufacturer coupon and applicable Walgreens coupon(s) for the purchase of a single item, unless prohibited by either coupon offer.

• The coupon amount must be reduced if it exceeds the value of the item after other discounts or coupons are applied. (For example, a $5.00 coupon for a $4.99 item will result in a $4.99 coupon value).

• When purchasing multiple items, Walgreens accepts multiple identical coupons for multiple qualifying items as long as there is sufficient stock to satisfy other customers, unless a limit is specified.

Register Rewards Loyalty Program

• Walgreens issues Register Rewards with certain items as a promotion. For example, $3 Register Rewards back for a $10 Pampers purchase. Generally, Register Rewards expire within two weeks of being issue. These may not be combined with another manufacturer's coupon.

Competitor Coupons Policy

• Walgreens does not accept competitor coupons.

Internet Coupons Policy

• Walgreens accepts valid internet/print at home coupons.

Sale Items

• Walgreens will accept manufacturer coupons for an item that is on sale. In the event that any item's selling price is less than the value of the coupon, Walgreens will only accept the coupon in exchange for the selling price of the item. Coupon redemption can never exceed the selling price of an item and no cash back is ever provided in exchange for any coupons.

CVS Coupon Policy

ExtraCare Rewards Program

CVS has a rewards system called "Extra Bucks" where they give you coupons for discounts and cash off at the bottom of your receipt.

You'll need an ExtraCare card to take advantage of all of the sales and discounts, but the program is free and easy to join. For more about the ExtraCare Rewards Program, or to sign up, go to www.cvs.com/CVSApp/user/extracare/extracare.jsp.

Double Coupons Policy

CVS Coupons are redeemed at face value only.

Stacking Coupons Policy

CVS allows one (1) store coupon and one (1) manufacturer coupon per item. You may also use your Extra Care Bucks (ECB) in combination with other coupons.

Unless a limit is specified, CVS accepts multiple like coupons for multiple qualifying items as long as there is sufficient stock to satisfy other customers.

Competitor Coupons Policy

CVS does not accept competitor coupons.

Internet Coupons Policy

CVS accepts coupons printed from the Internet as long as they have a barcode that scans at the register.

Coupons on Sale Items

CVS will accept manufacturer coupons for an item that is on sale.

CVS will not accept percent off coupons for sale and promotional items.

In the event that any item's price is less than the value of the coupon, CVS will accept the coupon only to the price of the item (no cash back).

The coupon amount will be reduced if it exceeds the value of the item after other discounts or coupons are applied. (For example, a $5.00 coupon for a $4.99 item will result in a $4.99 coupon value).

Kroger Coupon Policy

General Coupons Policy

• Kroger is in the process of drafting an official coupon policy. Check the company's website for updates or discuss the policies with the manager of your local store.

Double Coupons Policy

• Coupon doubling policies vary by region. For example, the Dallas/Fort Worth, Houston, Northern Kentucky, Cincinnati, Dayton, West Tennessee, Mississippi, Arkansas, Southern Missouri and Southwest Kentucky no longer double coupons at all.

• In most of the other locations, manufacturer coupons of $0.50 or less will be doubled every day. Manufacturer coupons of $0.51-$1.00 will be redeemed for $1.00 and manufacturer coupons over $1.00 will be redeemed at face value.

Stacking Coupons Policy

• Limit one (1) manufacturer coupon per item.

• Kroger no longer permits customers to stack e-coupons with paper manufacturer coupons.

Competitor Coupons Policy

• Kroger does not accept any competitor coupons for grocery items.

• Kroger accepts competitor coupons only for prescriptions in the pharmacy department (for example, a $5 Rite Aid gift card for a transferred prescription).

Digital Coupons Policy (loaded to your Kroger Plus Card)

• Customers choosing to participate in the digital coupons are required to have an active online account with a valid, associated shopper card.

Albertsons Coupon Policy

General Coupons Policy

Coupons stating "on next/future purchase or visit" cannot be used in the transaction in which they are generated. Next purchase is defined as a separate transaction.

The coupon redemption value on 'Free' coupons may not exceed the value of the item.

Store Coupons Policy

Coupons issued by Albertsons contain redemption guidelines including, but not limited to: "terms of agreement," "face value," "expiration date" and the words "store coupon."

Albertsons offers store coupons in various forms of media: electronic, newspaper, direct mailers, kiosks and company websites.

Store coupons may require that the discount apply only with Preferred/Loyalty/Rewards Card use.

Rain checks for store coupons will be given out as long as the store coupon does not state on it "while supplies last."

Manufacturer Coupons Policy

Coupons issued by manufacturers contain redemption guidelines including, but not limited to: "terms of agreement," "face value," "expiration date," and the words "manufacturer coupon."

Albertsons adheres to all manufacturer redemption guidelines. Albertsons may issue private promotion "manufacturer coupons" in advertisements that state "redeemable only at Albertsons" in which Albertsons is the only retailer that will accept.

Coupons that exceed the retail value of an item will be adjusted to provide the maximum value, not exceeding the price of the item.

Stacking Coupons Policy

Albertsons will accept one (1) manufacturer coupon and one (1) store coupon on the same qualifying item.

Double Coupons Policy

Twice the Value store coupons can only be used in combination with a $1.00 or less. Manufacturer coupon (a printed face value of $1.01 or greater) cannot be combined with Twice the Value store coupons.

Albertsons DOES allow manufacturer coupons that state they cannot be 'doubled' to be used in conjunction with a Twice the Value store coupon.

Competitor Coupons Policy

Albertsons does not accept competitor coupons. (Coupons generated by any competitor with competitor logo are considered competitor coupons.)

Internet Coupons Policy

Albertsons accepts Internet-generated manufacturer coupons as long as they clearly indicate that they are a manufacturer coupon and have a valid manufacturer address printed on them. The coupons must have a redemption value less than $5, have serial numbers and scan at checkout.

Albertsons will not accept Internet-generated manufacturer coupons that offer a free product without a required purchase.

www.ingramcontent.com/pod-product-compliance
Lightning Source LLC
Chambersburg PA
CBHW071159220526
45468CB00003B/1085